mommy Dreams

finding hope for the longings of your heart

IBS
PUBLISHING

Nov. 2000

from Michelle W.

Mommy Dreams

Developed in partnership with MOPS International
Compiled by Brenda Quinn
Designed by Jennifer Philips

IBS
PUBLISHING
1820 Jet Stream Drive
Colorado Springs, Colorado 80921
800/524-1588

Selections NIV-4110
IBS 99-20000

Printed in U.S.A.
12/99

Maybe you always dreamed of being a mom. You were the little girl who couldn't wait to replace dolls with real babies. You dreamed of cradling your own children in your arms and laughing with them as they grew.

Or maybe you didn't think too much about being a mother until you'd nearly become one. Yet when that child came into your life, motherhood touched you as nothing ever had. The strength of your love was surprising, the intensity of emotion indescribable.

While the dreaming and the love never cease, every mom soon discovers that motherhood involves more than cradles and laughter. It is also made up of long days, weary nights and endless questions about how best to love. For some, the struggles seem to engulf the joy. Motherhood catapults us to heights unimagined, and depths unexplored.

In these heights and depths, many of us can't help but sense the presence of God—the Creator of life and a Being who is greater, and much more capable, than we are. Despite being the parent now, the caregiver, we feel more in need of his help than ever.

God shares our moments of maternal ecstasy . . . and of desperation. He understands, and he offers help. Through the words of real-life mothers, this book will likely echo some of your reflections on motherhood. And it will respond with many words from God himself about how he feels toward you, how his heart so closely resembles the heart of a mother. Those words (the ones in italic) are found in the Bible, a timeless message from the living, loving Keeper of dreams.

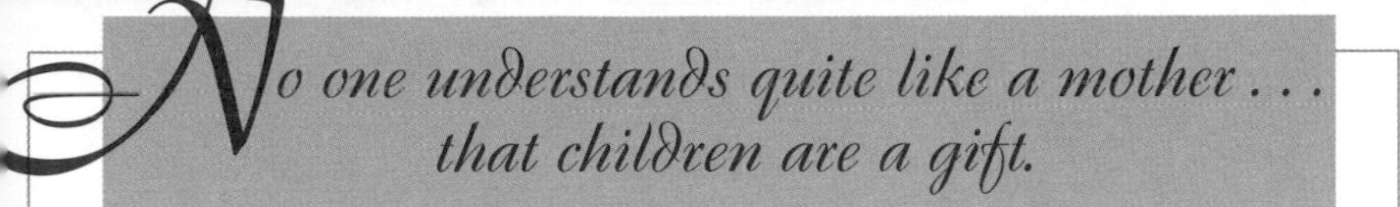

1

"God gives us beautiful gifts.
For me, one is being a mother."

Every good and perfect gift is from above, coming down from the Father of the heavenly lights, who does not change like shifting shadows. He chose to give us birth through the word of truth, that we might be a kind of firstfruits of all he created.

"No one could have prepared me for this. Nothing I had read or seen could describe the exquisite joy of my soul. 'I'm a mother!' Me! Oh, heart, be still. Who is this sweet face—so fresh from heaven—peeking out from beneath her blanket cocoon?

O God, you have such faith and trust in me. Please stay close and whisper in my ear the things I need to know. I want to do my best."

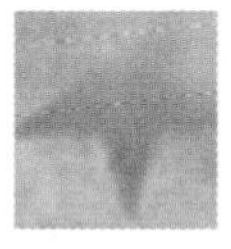

The angel said to her, "Do not be afraid, Mary, you have found favor with God. You will be with child and give birth to a son, and you are to give him the name Jesus."

And Mary said: "My soul glorifies the Lord and my spirit rejoices in God my Savior, for he has been mindful of the humble state of his servant. From now on all generations will call me blessed, for the Mighty One has done great things for me—holy is his name." . . . And she gave birth to her firstborn, a son. . . . Mary treasured up all these things and pondered them in her heart.

"When was the magical day, the one when
I became a mother? I'm not sure if it was the day my son
was born, or the first time he said that enchanted word
'Mommy.' I think the reason I can't remember the specific
moment I became a mother is because it's impossible to
imagine not being one."

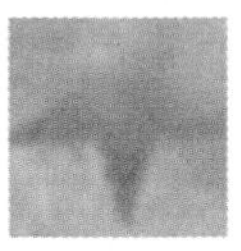

Be strong and courageous. Do not be afraid . . .

for the LORD your God goes with you;

he will never leave you nor forsake you.

"I never imagined the beauty of motherhood
until you arrived. The way you get lost in my eyes
sharing those love-filled moments when you smile at me,
curl up to me, cry for me; watching you sleeping,
being there when you awaken. I'm so thankful to God
for having every day with you."

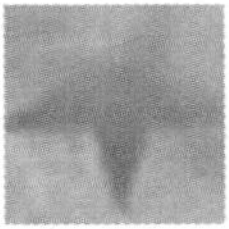

People were bringing little children to Jesus to have him touch them, but the disciples rebuked them. When Jesus saw this, he was indignant. He said to them, "Let the little children come to me, and do not hinder them, for the kingdom of heaven belongs to such as these. I tell you the truth, anyone who will not receive the kingdom of God like a little child will never enter it." And he took the children in his arms, put his hands on them and blessed them.

“While expecting, I was always told my life would be so different, but no one ever said how much better it would be.”

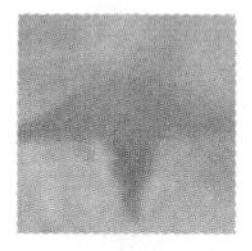

“Raising a child—teaching, encouraging,
disciplining—through all of this, does he know
I love him? This morning I received my answer.
My rambunctious toddler crawled into my lap and,
laying the sweetest of kisses on my cheek,
said, ‘Momma, you’re my best friend.’
My heart is still singing.”

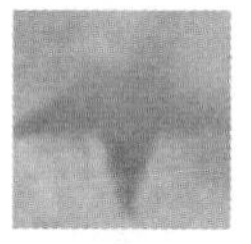

I have seen you in the sanctuary and beheld your power and your glory. Because your love is better than life, my lips will glorify you. I will praise you as long as I live, and in your name I will lift up my hands. My soul will be satisfied as with the richest of foods; with singing lips my mouth will praise you. On my bed I remember you; I think of you through the watches of the night. Because you are my help, I sing in the shadow of your wings.

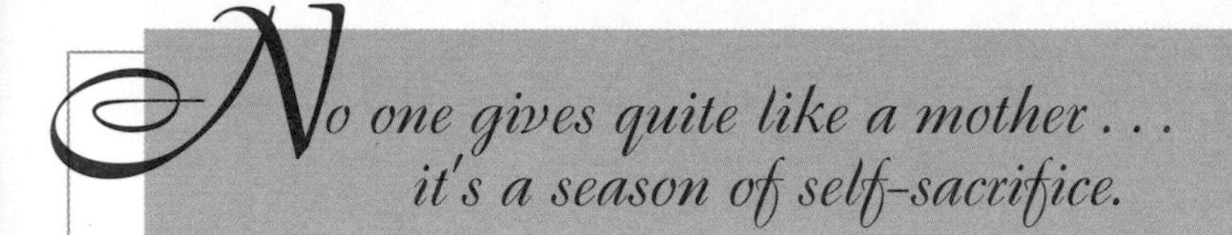

2

"My baby takes up all of my day—
and all of myself."

Come to me all you who are weary and burdened,

and I will give you rest.

"Being a young single mom is filled with tough times;
pushing myself to cook dinner when I'm too tired
to stand; having to go to the store for milk
when I'm too sick to get up; worrying all night
because my little one has such a high fever,
knowing I have to go to work the next day."

"Most of my friends work,
so there's no time for friendship,
except at night when I'm too tired."

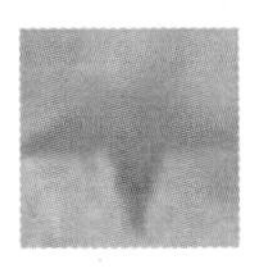

You are my hiding place;

you will protect me from trouble

and surround me with songs of deliverance.

Let us not give up meeting together . . . ,

but let us encourage one another.

The Lord, the Lord, is my strength and my song;

he has become my salvation.

"My kids place their food and drink orders all day. My husband stays after work to have a beer, comes home, eats and goes to bed. I feel like no one thought of me at all the whole day."

You know when I sit and when I rise; you perceive my thoughts from afar. You discern my going out and my lying down; you are familiar with all my ways. Before a word is on my tongue you know it completely, O Lord.

Such knowledge is too wonderful for me, too lofty for me to attain. Where can I go from your Spirit? Where can I flee from your presence? If I go up to the heavens, you are there; if I make my bed in the depths, you are there. If I rise on the wings of the dawn, if I settle on the far side of the sea, even there your hand will guide me, your right hand will hold me fast. . . .

For you created my inmost being; you knit me together in my mother's womb. I praise you because I am fearfully and wonderfully made; your works are wonderful, I know that full well. . . . All the days ordained for me were written in your book before one of them came to be. How precious to me are your thoughts, O God! How vast is the sum of them!

"Day after day, there is no time for me!"

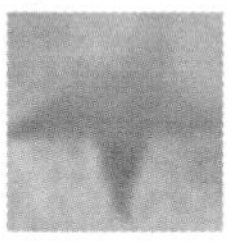

He gives strength to the weary and increases the power of the weak. . . . Those who hope in the LORD will renew their strength. They will soar on wings like eagles; they will run and not grow weary, they will walk and not be faint.

"I used to play tennis and be active,
but now I'm out of shape."

Everyone who competes in the games goes into strict training. They do it to get a crown that will not last; but we do it to get a crown that will last forever.

A wife of noble character who can find?
She is worth far more than rubies.

She selects wool and flax and works with eager hands.

She gets up while it is still dark; she provides food
for her family and portions for her servant girls.

She sets about her work vigorously;
her arms are strong for her tasks.

She opens her arms to the poor and

extends her hands to the needy.

She is clothed with strength and dignity; she can laugh at the days to come. She speaks with wisdom, and faithful instruction is on her tongue. She watches over the affairs of her household and does not eat the bread of idleness. Her children arise and call her blessed; her husband also, and he praises her:

"Many women do noble things,

but you surpass them all."

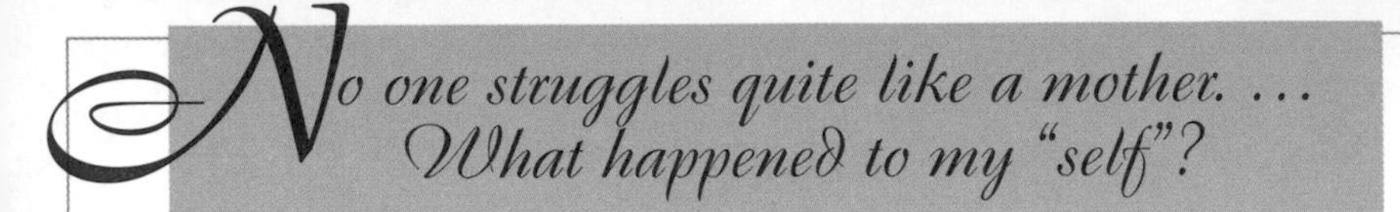

No one struggles quite like a mother. . . . What happened to my "self"?

3

"I'm about 99 percent mom and only 1 percent myself."

"I used to be able to handle an important career,
run a home, and be a reasonably good wife,
so I naturally assumed I would be just as effective
in mothering. I simply wasn't prepared for this
downward spiral of my own self-worth."

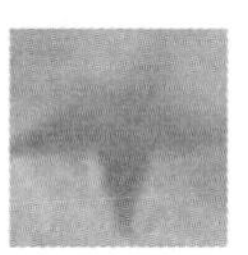

Ah, Sovereign LORD, you have made the heavens and the earth by your great power and outstretched arm. Nothing is too hard for you.

"I'm not who I thought I was.
I wanted to be a perfect mom."

Your hands made me and formed me;
give me understanding.

"All I talk about these days is potty-this and potty-that."

"I feel strange now when I go out without the kids (which is rare) . . . like I'm not as important alone."

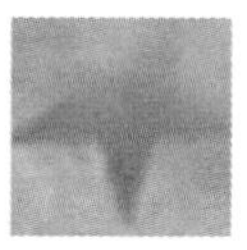

The LORD is my shepherd, I shall not be in want.

He makes me lie down in green pastures,

he leads me beside quiet waters, he restores my soul.

He guides me in paths of righteousness

for his name's sake. Even though I walk

through the valley of the shadow of death,

I will fear no evil, for you are with me;
your rod and your staff, they comfort me.
You prepare a table before me in the presence
of my enemies. You anoint my head with oil;
my cup overflows. Surely goodness and love
will follow me all the days of my life, and
I will dwell in the house of the LORD forever.

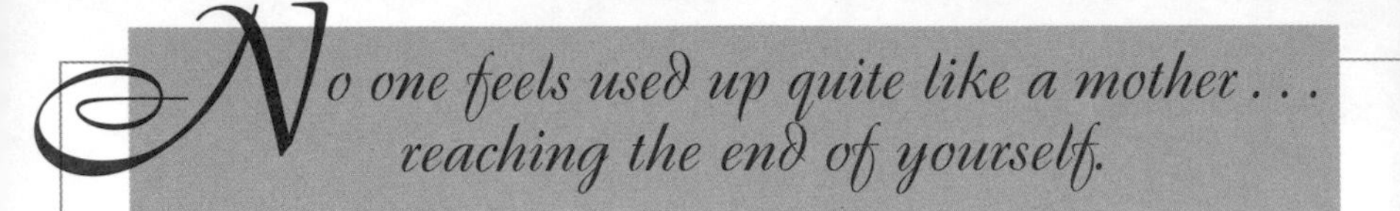

4

"Being a mom requires such patience and self-control. My first response is to screech, but I can't teach my children patience and self-control if I'm showing the opposite."

The fruit of the Spirit is love, joy, peace, patience, kindness, goodness, faithfulness, gentleness and self-control.

"Why is it I can never finish anything? There are always noses to wipe, spills to mop up, tears to dry. I know there will come a day when my house will be clean, a time when I can walk from room to room without tripping over toys, or hearing the endless bickering between kids. But then, I'll probably miss it."

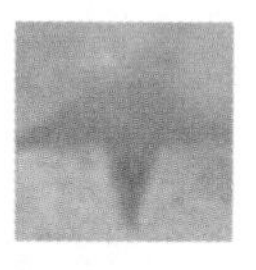

Because of the LORD's great love we are not consumed, for his compassions never fail.

“Keeping up with the kids isn’t the hardest part of mothering; it’s the loneliness.”

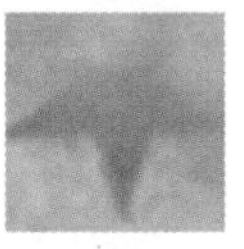

How long, O LORD? Will you forget me forever?

How long will you hide your face from me?

How long must I wrestle with my thoughts

and every day have sorrow in my heart?

How long will my enemy triumph over me?

Look on me and answer, O LORD my God.

Give light to my eyes, or I will sleep in death ...

But I trust in your unfailing love; my heart

rejoices in your salvation. I will sing to the LORD,

for he has been good to me.

God asks: *Can a mother forget the baby at her breast and have no compassion on the child she has borne? Though she may forget, I will not forget you! See, I have engraved you on the palm of my hands. . . .*

"Today I feel shocked and angry that the kids are so demanding. It seems like they are trying to torture me. Can't they tell I need some space, time to think, time to put the house in some semblance of order? Don't they know that I can't do two things at once? Can't they just go five minutes without a request? How can it be that they need me so much?"

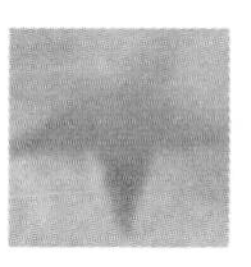

This is what the LORD says—he who made you,
who formed you in the womb, and who will help you:
Do not be afraid. . . . For I will pour water on the
thirsty land, and streams on the dry ground;
I will pour out my Spirit on your offspring.

"Today I forgot to pick up my child at the bus stop. I can't believe I did that! Keeping up with a family, a job, and my own life is tiring. I try, but sometimes I don't feel like I'm a very good mom."

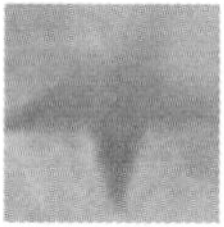

My peace I give you. I do not give to you as the world gives. Do not let your hearts be troubled and do not be afraid.

"So much of our success in life, after all, is measured by how well we are able to get through the times that aren't so good—the times when we're too tired, when we're frightened, when we fail. If we are not around to serve as examples for our children, for how to get through those times and emerge victorious, then how will they learn the lesson? Few of us really are 'born' for the job of mothering.... It means being willing to confront the worst in ourselves and being brave enough not to run away from it."

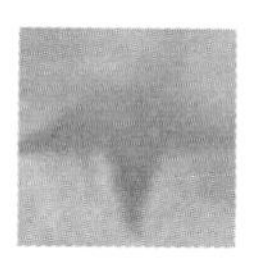

Praise be to the God . . . who comforts us in all our troubles, so that we can comfort those in any trouble with the comfort we ourselves have received from God.

Do not fear, for I am with you; do not be dismayed, for I am your God. I will strengthen you and help you; I will uphold you.

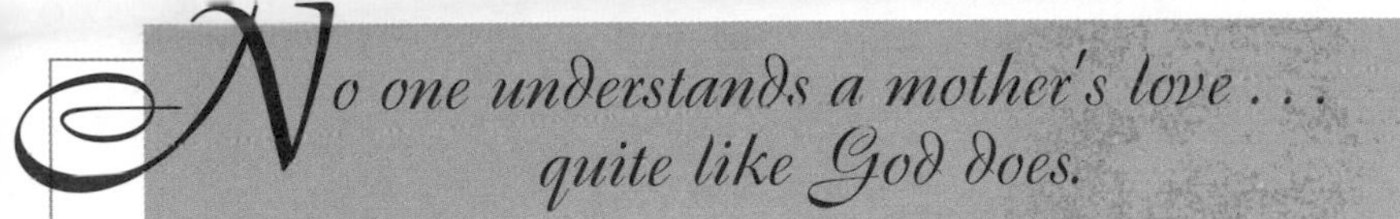

5

"Oh, my little one, I'd give my life for you."

For God so loved the world that he gave his one and only Son, that whoever believes in him shall not perish but have eternal life. For God did not send his Son into the world to condemn the world, but to save the world through him.

As a mother comforts her child,

so I will comfort you. ... When you see this,

your heart will rejoice.

"Disciplining my children is difficult for me because I hate conflict. I have to remind myself that teaching my children to mind will save them from a lot of heartache in the long run. Allowing them not to obey is cruel."

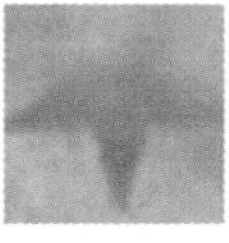

Train a child in the way he should go,
and when he is old he will not turn from it.

Hear, O Israel: The LORD our God, the LORD is one.
Love the LORD your God with all your heart and
with all your soul and with all your strength.
These commandments that I give you today are to
be upon your hearts. Impress them on your children.
Talk about them when you sit at home and when
you walk along the road, when you lie down
and when you get up.

"I want to be liked by my children, and it's very hard to accept when sometimes I'm not."

"It is difficult to draw that fine line between loving and nurturing my children and smothering and overprotecting them. I'm constantly trying to keep that balance in check, which becomes difficult because it's a constant questioning of my mothering ability."

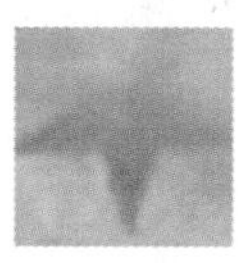

I will instruct you and teach you

in the way you should go;

I will counsel you and watch over you.

"Oh, how I love to hold my little ones close especially when they're sad, touching their hair or faces, rocking them back and forth. Isn't it amazing how no one ever has to teach a mother how to comfort her own child?"

He tends his flock like a shepherd:

He gathers the lambs in his arms

and carries them close to his heart;

he gently leads those that have young.

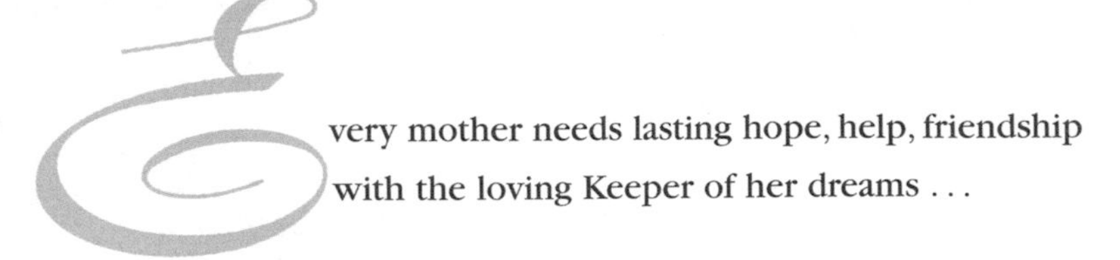

very mother needs lasting hope, help, friendship with the loving Keeper of her dreams . . .

God is the greatest hope any mother could find. He holds our dreams and offers a secure place to come with our joys, our frustrations, our inadequacies. God isn't hard to find—like a mother, he waits with open arms and a full heart.

If you'd like to get to know him better, talk with a friend who knows him. Read the Bible. Ask God for help. He has the answers for your life as a mom. He holds your family's future.

See, I have engraved you on the palm of my hands. . . .

MOPS International

MOPS stands for Mothers of Preschoolers, a program designed for mothers with children under school age. Approximately 2,000 MOPS groups meet in churches throughout the United States, Canada, and 11 other countries touching the needs of more than 80,000 moms each year. The women are of many ages and backgrounds, but share the same desire—to be the best mothers they can be. To find out if there is a MOPS group near you, or to learn about resources MOPS offers to support you, find us at our Web site, http://www.MOPS.org or call 303-733-5353 or 800-929-1287. To learn how to start a MOPS group, call 1-888-910-6677.

Better moms make a better world!

Scripture References

James 1:17–18
Luke 1:30–31,46–49; 2:7a,19
Deuteronomy 31:6
Mark 10:13–16
Psalm 63:2–7
Matthew 11:28
Psalm 32:7; Hebrews 10:25
Isaiah 12:2b
Psalm 139:2–4,6–10,13–14,16b–17
Isaiah 40:29–31
1 Corinthians 9:25
Proverbs 31:10,13,15,17,20,25–29
Jeremiah 32:17
Psalm 119:73
Psalm 23
Galatians 5:22
Lamentations 3:22
Psalm 13:1–3,5–6
Isaiah 49:15-16a
Isaiah 44:2–3
John 14:27
2 Corinthians 1:3–4; Isaiah 41:10
John 3:16–17
Isaiah 66:13–14a
Proverb 22:6; Deuteronomy 6:4–7
Psalm 32:8
Isaiah 40:11
Isaiah 49:16